AF265348

Reflections of an Indigo Soul

Reflections of an Indigo Soul

Please Digest!

Yasnary Contreras

<u>**Special thanks**</u>

The self I have yet to uncover,

(God) = For sending people and situations that reveal my purpose in this plane of existence….for allowing me to be a master teacher in disguise.

Zahara Contreras (Daughter) for being my greatest lesson, and my best friend, I love you beyond understanding.

Krystal Harrow -my (spiritual sister)= I can't begin to thank you for showing me the way

Rose Whaley -(Teacher-advisor)-For reminding me who I really am, for your unconditional support and lessons full of awareness. Thank you for your vision

To the many individuals that came into my line of vision and aided my growth, Emily Warren for allowing me to write without expectations.

Contents

Zahara, take it and run with it!!!

LOVE

      LOVE

LOVE

       LOVE

         LOVE

      LOVE

LOVE   *LOVE*

      LOVE

LOVE

Ode to mother earth

The day that you shed rain on me mother it was the day my soul you freed, with all your intensity, there I stood to receive life at its truest. Standing there something I conceived light so bright for all to see, in the past when I walked in the dark, energy in my heart you would spark, as if to say, "taste, taste this fruit that for you I have made." You brought to life all things, destroying in me all things that would sting, bringing me back to the basics, now I'm in control, manipulating all the things that EGO once stole. You helped me remember to LOVE ALL THE THINGS THAT I AM, the one insect to bring back food for her friends, the water that supports life in a plants stem, the flexibility that allows a ruler to bend, even the ink in a pen that aided many poets to write with no end. I AM THAT I AM because of you. So many things you granted me in my youth.

Still I stood that in the park when the wind blew so strong and true, revealing to me series of past truths. She said,

"NEVER DID I GO, I BRING KNOWLEDGE TO ALL WHO WANT TO KNOW; NOTHING IS NEW, NOTHING IS NEW I AM COMPOUND OF ALL THAT IS, NOTHING IS NEW NOTHING IS NEW."

This mother EARTH is my ode to you…

Reasons why I write

I write, I write because the blood that flows
through your brain needs some resuscitation, I
write because I'm you, I write because I need a
band of idiots to live my words, I write because
my words compose reality, negatively and
positively, I write for all the reasons you don't, for
the one nail stuck on the wall, for the four-year old
lost at the mall.
I write for the words that dance on bathroom stalls.
These are the reasons I write,
I write for the seasons,
For the hate with no reason,
For the love that was forgotten
For the ink my pen sustains,
I write because I write
I write because I write for the blind,
And the blinds that cover the sunlight,
I write for the bottle that sustains my water,
I write for the little boy, who said he will sell my
daughters hair for CIGARRETES,
I write with reasons,
For stolen memories….I write for unfound
treasures and for those lost in translations.

I write because the words flow through me, I write because I am the MESSENGER and my duty is to deliver. I write for the many little bones that compose a hand, I write for you and your friend, for reality with no end, I write because I am the great composer and am made of compositions, I write because I birth a poem today, I write because writing is my voyage to my Christ mind.
These are the reasons why I write……

PLEASE DIGEST

The messenger

Here I come to relate the message; here I come with this galactic force that I have mirrored from all that your *SPIRIT* is.

I came here now to replant the seed that was covered by the *VEIL* placed upon this breed, now help me succeed, help me and your soul I will feed. *OVERSTAND* I brought the message from the 12th dimension, please don't turn about face I don't have bad intentions. Though I know a little weird I may seem, overstand it's all a *SCHEME* the *ILLUSION* that you're living keeps sucking all your *ENERGY*. Check the books it's the PROPHECY, the end of this age has come, so that means that soon your stage is gone, seek help from the CRYSTALLIZE they will help you metamorphosis, and the INDIGOS they have come and gone in the early stages of this earth and will be here to aid humanity, the ones that are here now and yes the ones that are about to come.
I AM THAT I AM ONE with *GOD*, and as god I'm *DIVINE* and like my sisters the stars I shine. Let me help you elevate and *ASCEND* because only deeper consciousness will help you MEND loose ends.
Though history portrays fear and pain, overstand it's just your higher self they been trying to tame.
Don't be a shame don't you see it's all a game.
Something certified in this earth is change, this is our global revolution and like change we can't stop

evolution. I came here to relate the message higher consciousness is the resolution to knock down this crucial man made global institution, destitution, prostitution of the mind can't and won't ever allow you to be divine but don't worry there would be a time that with the CRYSTALLIZE and the INDIGOS we shall dine.
Peace, *love* and *harmony* will be the only symphony; this will help you find yourself and your TRINITY

Time

The illusion of space and time is an empty void that attracts puppets of self destruction into a vortex of crafted sceneries. Time is nothing but a fictional concept keeping beauty on a rhythmic death row, pushing the limits **of life into a state of nothingness**

Death of blank pages

Never embrace blank pages.
Touch the thought that relies on opinions sit it down and invite it to a cup of tea. Let it be holistic and perhaps holy like that of the scriptures of past souls. Nevertheless let him gather the stars and sacrifice his heart, for he knows believe me he does. Continue, feel like you must cancel that dream and let the gun blast and awake the sarcasm that takes over and goes to war with his insides, let it shed it skins, let it crawl and dig in the encounters of the world, it would change who you used to be the old you will dangle and collide with every bough that tried to make it through the storm. Let him drown while he counts the leaves on a tree and he shall swim only if he's a believer he will not sleep.

The Invitation

I lay my head on your chest and go on to
pursue your thundering beat. It finds me
feeling naïve and gullible yet in a spiritual
ecstasy. Every pound invited me to a feast of
things unknown.

First it detoxified me,

Then it enriched me with innocence soon
thereafter it washed me with love, taught me
that poison kills,

That the flesh of a worm was
tougher than a human, and
that our worst enemy is
darkness.

I kissed your chest ever so
softly spreading love to my
new kingdom,

I look into your eyes and see
myself dressed in

Purity,

Baptized in wisdom,

Carved from knowledge,
Sentenced to overstanding,
then I truly over-stood that I was
A woman from the tribe of the messiah

::::::::::::

The Revolution IS YOU

This system of the dead is left for the dead..........

WAKE UP!!!

Lost words

Where would my words go?
On walls or in bathroom stalls, on sweaters or
on hallmark letters in train stations or your
imagination, how many people will see them,
how many people will believe them, on ceilings
or amidst some bodies feelings. Would they
cause a revolution or simply give a solution.

Where would my words go?

Where would they go?

If your eyes go would you want it in Braille
codes?

In this life geniuses are born every day, what
else do you need me to say, what do you need a
hearing aid?

Where would my words go?

Where would they go?

Would it give life to empty vessels or would they
die on this

PLANTATION???

Prophesied in Spanish.........

Mi lapicero,

Soldado valiente es
Poeta soy yo,
Como el viento bueno
Sonadora tambien
Igual que la paloma.
Me quieres conocer hoy?
Soy la solitud que camina
Contigo.
Me reconoces?
Illumino tus noches
Te brindo amor.
Mi linda mariposa
Fresca y fina
Si desnudas tu amor
guardare tu luz
En el cielo magico
Y cuando llueva
Tu alas oiran y la guerra pararan
Serpientes saldran
Pendiente a tus vozes
Conciente reiran al saber
Que son libres
A ti honaran
Aprenderan a sonar
Me restirare
Alcansar lo maximo a
Otro mundo
El cual es ideal

The hidden

Like an interrogation room, the reflection on the mirror shows the infections of the words that have been lost in translation   so, So I feel so lost on this dimension, The mental deficit caused by insurrection carcasses of the baby boom, pursuing their mistakes amongst this room, Sensation room, the illusion room that was created to sedate our senses. So the master fed his beast with thoughts that were resurrected from ancient books, with the outlook of production of mental destruction. The Buddha should have stayed longer to disallow the intruder,

To disallow being "Jewed" of, Of our conscious,

Which many people believe to be priceless.

"TODAY I LIVED THE TRUTH, WHAT DID YOU DO"

Girl with the purple hair

I am more than that girl with the purple hair,

more than that girl with the *BLEEDING EYES.*

I am more than that girl with the *BROKEN*

SMILE; I am more than *STORIES PAST*. I am

more than the girl with a *WET HOLE, A*

SILENT SOUL; I am more than the

SPEECHLESS GIRL. I am more than the girl

with the *Purple* **hair.**

Louder Than Words

Amidst of silence there's a roaring noise, but even amongst this noise there's an inexplicable silence this is where I am. Within the silence of this noise....the walls that construct it become my crouches and the flames my food, the anger my sanity and as this silence becomes shattered the stinging memories die away>>>>>>>>>>>>>

She signs: From someone who knows

She signs from
someone who knows…

She goes on intellectually decapitating all sceneries,

Though it wasn't the "lady in red" she usually danced
to, beauty knew to maintain her composure every where
she went she was sure to.

She favors the color green, giving life to all dead things.
Her spirit brings springs of water quenching the life
thirst you been experiencing.

All the differences beauty makes in a day, trust me that
with you they would stay, making your day with
something as simple as "HEY ARE YOU OKAY."

The 2 year old bacon slowly digesting in my mind
makes me recall all of those funny times.

The physically far, close to my heart you are. I see you
all around me, when I look at my daughter she reminds
me, of the decision made, **a decision that has
blessed me for the rest of my days.**

**She portrays wildflowers spiritually guided by
all the powers around her. I'm looking around
saying "damn, where did I find her," not
realizing she found me, helped me revive the**

beauty that was slowly vanishing. Gave me love
that was distracting all the challenges I was drowning
in.

So today I stand a soldier valiant in the battle field with
love in hands....

THANK YOU to the beauty that signs:

FROM SOMEONE WHO KNOWS

Memories of the Unfound

Carnival at 6:30, head or tails, duck duck goose, water balloons, 5 black bags of candy, pigeon poop, snow angel, ripped stocking, writing hated, math obsessed, math hated, writing in love, secrets, whispering, dreamt falling of roof, the dawn is peaceful, 5:30, school boring, construction of words on candy wrappers never exposed. Music must seek, must be where I'm required to be, in the wind with the words that once took me around the world. Patience and time, every twist, every hair lock, in the position he sat that would once attract words of torture words of paradise. Human's constructions that distracts, Wisdom, pharaohs, Ethiopians, Egyptian hey wait but this is not about religion. Smile on my face to know that I'm not really going anywhere with this. Screw it back to religion, was Jesus a demigod, prophet or really the sanctified. Where is this hero called Jesus, is this when philosophy metaphors and poetry turn into one or break up in multitudes like fiber optics, misplace and replace the supposed un-place-able.

Butterflies and the garden that disinfected the cruelty that was never swell. Where is the child playing hide and seek anticipating the time she can't sneak twirling and laughing under the bed, damn! I was found; disillusion never ends its horrible how this story ends strings of colorful lines blackened by the tint of my dark blue jeans.

"Time is often the deity of space and lies of the truth. Though its immortality is promised its core is deceased."

Yasnary Contreras

Poetic soul

Dance poetic soul,

Dance with your sincere love for words dance, nobody can knock down your stance,

Dance beautiful soul dance; let the bow and arrow of your spirit penetrate every cell of your body,

Let the double helix of your DNA multiply, so that it may paint and design true reality,

words of affirmation, let it wash down to future generations,

Revive your tribe of poetic souls,

Dance poetic soul, DANCE,

Let the sweat running down your flesh nourish all things that have been desensitize, allowing them to return to their state of nature,

Relive true meditation,

DANCE POETIC SOUL…….DANCE!!!

"When you take a moment to carefully look at your surroundings you find beauty in the ugly, direction in the lost, peace in the noise love in the hate and joy in the anger"

-Yasnary Contreras

For the children

Give me a poem for the children God;
give me a poem for the children.

Let their ears flourish from the
foundations of their brain, so that I may
extend with courage and strength the
living vibrations that come across as
wave lengths.

Give me a poem for the children God,
give me a torch of light and a heart full of
might, so that may convey all the things
you would want me to say.

Tell them how life is beautiful in every
single way, how the sun that shines
above them enables DNA, remind them
that they are God and Goddesses from a
land far away coming here to make a
difference every day.

Feed me with your thoughts God so I that
I may translate truth with a regurgitation
of your love.

Give me a paintbrush so that I may cover
all the stains and bruises that in their
heart remains.

Sometimes parents do the best they can,
though in your perception it may not be
enough trust me, you chose them it' s
exactly what you needed in order to
grow!!!

In the thralldom

Society promised an illusion that tarnished our souls

Sold us a dream, to engage our minds in actions that were deceiving to our person

We were sold a dream a dream of success, but instead we were put out in fields where monsters lingered, drank and cheered at our falling tears.

We were sold dreams, dreams wished we could return

We were chosen,

Chosen

and chosen again.

We reeked of fear,

Caressed

embarrassment, Relieved

deception, and drank rage...

The world doesn't save, hasn't saved and will never save only true consciousness can help you ascend...

PLEASE

DIGEST.....

"Why is it that those who think they are free are the ones actually enslaved; too sad to see so challenging to save."

—Yasnary Contreras

*"I lent him my eyes
hoping he could see but
instead he became more
blind…*

*How do you expect to
learn if your not receptive
to it?"*

-YASNARY.C.

The Epiphany

Woke up this morning didn't like what I see, all the people
of the world killing themselves slowly, self mutilation in
most situations, from scorching hot showers, through
piercings, simply believing we have the power…perceiving
themselves to be the truest they can be, with no recollection
or premeditation of their self destruction and faulty
construction of a fake reality. The poem-emcees dropped to
their knees, love letters turned into tarnished walls, hurt
took place in the eyes of men. Disconnected, translated into
hatred, our thoughts molested, by the incarnation of the
desecrated,,, hidden messages in the English language,
believe lied, hate ate all the beautiful things we are, here we
stand in disarray, indulging in materialism every day,,
repetitive notions prostitute the mouth of man… spoken
emotions are claimed to be the jail of humans,, as if
feeling was a crime. Time and times again
people hide from themselves only running
and creating hell.

PLEASE DIGEST!!

The Copy and Paste

These days I the circle amongst squares become impatient. Fighting and altercations surround my world. Though it is not I with the clenched fist their spirit still rubs on me. Their spewing anger attaches on me like leeches, their ignorance perpetrates their devastating experiences and the essence of their lost state barricades their souls and I the circle amongst squares grow edges…my emotions in a box I grow four sides trapping myself with every angle…I guess even angels can become quadrilaterals.

For the sleeping goddesses

Look at me I am black, some say I see some say I see not, some say I see **NOT**. The knots of my assumed dumb down mind I uncoiled, feed my supreme thoughts that were manipulated and spoiled. Look at me, I am black, my womb the armor for the dis-eased, peace forth I will bring, with this thirst for knowledge I will outburst. I am the pure reflection of you DNA curls. You may judge and mistreat me but you seem to forget that I spend more time being **YOU**, speaking like **HIM**, learning like her, **LOVING** like **WE**. In your eyes I became a pupil, on your lips I read my life, in your hand you hold my disguise, in your hair the sound of my voice lies.

LOOK AT ME, I am BLACK some say **I SEE** some say **I SEE NOT**

A GODDESS Waiting
For the
GODDESS WITHIN

What are you waiting for???

Weary Shoes

MY shoes have a life span of
two months not because
they're cheap, but because
I'm always on the run. I'm a
runner yes indeed; a road
runner running at full speed.

Standing still is not an
option this is the reason why
running has become my best
distraction. At a standstill
you can smell the stench from
death, but is it really the
smell that throws you off or
is it because I am dead

The chosen Few

Leader Leader that you are lead, because those who will be lead are the foundation to the revolution. They will resuscitate the justice that's dead they are the lawless lawful here to strangulate deception before its time of its inception.

Leader leader that you are breathe life into us!!!!!!

The chosen must motivate,

The quiet must speak

And the lifeless must live awakened

Simple···

Feed mind, Feed
soul, Feed spirit,
Freed...... MIND,
Freed...... SOUL,
FREE......SPIRIT

As Yet Untitled,

Word's War,
Word's War, for the
living and the Poor,
for the stagnant
and the undecided
for those who are
spiritually divided

Recycled Story...

You told me, I told you, reflecting our reflection
on each other.

I am angered at your nonsense because you have
been crying wolf for years.

You cry the same cry, you shed the same tears...
tears that used to burn now they have become the
regular rainfall.

I am angered at the nonsense, your put downs your
ups and downs…

You have asked me to love myself now I ask you
to do the same, stop setting up these traps stop
dancing in hate's flame.

You have been beaten by life so much you now
master the same destruction creating a vicious
cycle you are drowning in your own self-
corruption.

It seems like your returning the favor, imbedding
in me your dying soul so that I can savor.

In the past month you have faced the same truth
different scenarios too many times.

Suddenly,

The girl you claim to have buried comes out with
patched up wounds;

Wounds I have intended to heal realizing I can't
break you out of your own cocoon

For Mental Starvation

This is dedicated for the mentally medicated for those who abandoned the real meaning their hearts once perpetrated. This is for the faithful faithless, for those whose heart's face is mutilated for those who ride on the back of hatred, for those who forgot God consciousness and in the process defecated on their soul with no redemption or feelings of disaster-ness this is for spiritual strangulation, for those whose mind lies in detention pushed down by this fake nation, for those whose philosophy is such a catastrophe; wake up and see what you're doing to us. The fumes that you breathe hurt you emotionally so you become full of stress to your past you regress with many regrets. This is for those who buried their voice and instead synchronized with a technological demise that keeps them brain dead and doesn't allow them to rise. This is for you your friend and that guy; please people open your eyes. You follow empty words or should I say killing swords that were only used by those who you crowned as lords. Please people open your eyes, please my brother and my sister please rise. Utilize the sacredness between your brow it's your heaven to the truth open your books now, notes to take

changes to make, the perfect ascension waiting at
hand, loose end to mend can you overstand open
your eyes I'm sure you can. I am asking you to
extend a hand on behalf of all the fallen men.

The Base Of
2…

Love

&

Fear

Fearlessness